This Journal Belongs To The Following Queen:

_____

"I love myself when I am laughing. . . and then again when I am looking
mean and impressive."
- Zora Neale Hurston

Made in the USA
Middletown, DE
16 March 2023

26936085R00060